Slow Cooker: 100% GLUTEN-FREE VEGAN! Irresistibly Good & Super Easy Gluten-Free Vegan Recipes for Slow Cooker

by Karen Greenvang

Contents

Introduction: Vegan Gluten-Free Recipes for the Slow Cooker

Gluten is a protein found in grains such as wheat, barley, rye and sometimes even oats. For those suffering from a gluten allergy, intolerance and the more serious coeliac disease, a diet that provides optimum nutrition and all your dietary needs has been very difficult to achieve in the past. This is because many commercially made foods contain fillers that are gluten based. Even the most common of condiments may contain maize starch, and anything that lists malt in its ingredients will be a gluten containing food.

Luckily the effects of gluten allergies, intolerances and coeliac disease have become better known to both consumers and manufacturers over the last few years, making gluten free options more available and more affordable than they previously were.

One of the best ways to manage such an allergy or intolerance is to take control of your meal planning and cook all your meals yourself. By taking this approach you are ensuring that you are consuming only the best quality ingredients and meals that are free from all of the additives and preservatives that are commonly found in commercially made convenience foods.

However, in the reality of our modern day fast paced lifestyles in which time is at a premium, spending hours in the kitchen cooking

1

is just not practical. This is where a slow cooker becomes an incredibly convenient tool. The safety and low energy consumption of a slow cooker means that you can prepare the ingredients of a dish the in advance and get your slow cooker going first thing in the morning before leaving for work so that your meal will be ready when you walk in the door at the end of the day. The slow cooker can also be left to cooking over night; allowing you to wake up in the morning to a delicious wholesome breakfast that requires little extra preparation.

Now you can begin preparing healthy, tasty and nutritious meals without any concern that you may be ingesting foods that don't fit into your chosen lifestyle. This book is divided into four sections, Breakfasts, Lunches, Dinners and Soups; and therefore provides you with many options.

Enjoy!

Free Complimentary eBook

Before we dive into the recipes, I would like to offer you a free, complimentary recipe eBook with delicious vegan superfood smoothies.

Download it now, before you forget:

www.bitly.com/karenfreegift

PART I Breakfasts

We all know that breakfast is the most important meal of the day, but some days things don't always go according to plan. We sleep through our alarm or spill toothpaste on our shirts, any number of unexpected things can happen during our morning rush that will result in running late and not having time for breakfast. This is where your slow cooker will really come to good use, by preparing your breakfast the night before and leaving the slow cooker to work its magic overnight, you will never have to worry about finding time to put breakfast together in the morning. The recipes in this section include high quality slow releasing carbohydrates, healthy fats and proteins that will help you kick start your day and your metabolism the healthy way.

Coconut Quinoa with Raspberries and Almonds

Quinoa is an incredibly versatile grain that is high in amino acids, essential minerals and is considered a complete protein, as well as being naturally gluten-free. Quinoa is also a slow-releasing high fiber carbohydrate, making it an excellent grain option for breakfast. Raspberries are high in antioxidants and vitamin C, they are also known for their cancer-fighting and anti-inflammatory properties. The coconut milk and almonds provide essential healthy fats and minerals.

Serves 4

Ingredients:

- 1 Cup (250ml) Raw quinoa

- 2 Cups (500ml) Coconut Milk

- 1 Cup (250ml) Fresh Raspberries

- 4 Tablespoons (60ml) Raw Almonds, roughly chopped

- 1 teaspoon (5ml) Ground cinnamon

- ½ teaspoon (2.5ml) Ground ginger

- 1 Cup (250ml) Coconut Cream, for serving

Instructions:

1. Place the raw quinoa in the dish of your slow cooker.

2. Add the ground cinnamon, ground ginger, raw almonds and fresh raspberries. Stir all together.

3. Add the coconut milk and stir well.

4. Place the lid on the slow cooker and set to low heat, leave to cook over night (approximately 8 hours)

To Serve:

1. In four separate serving bowls place ½ cup (125ml) of the cooked quinoa mix

2. Pour ¼ cup (60ml) of the coconut cream over each bowl and serve. If you have time, you can whip the coconut cream before placing it over the quinoa and sprinkling a little extra ground cinnamon over the top.

Banana Peanut Butter Gluten-Free Oatmeal with Raw Seeds

Oats are another great choice of grain for breakfast, especially in their whole form. Oats are high in slow-releasing carbohydrates and are known for their ability to help reduce cholesterol levels. You will be able to find gluten-free varieties of oatmeal in your local health store. Bananas are a great source of potassium and essential minerals, and the raw seeds add a dose of healthy omega 3 fats.

Serves 4

Ingredients:

- 1 Cup (250ml) Raw gluten-free oats

- 2 Cups (500ml) Oat milk

- 2 medium sized bananas, finely sliced

- 4 Tablespoons (60ml) Raw seed mix

- 1 teaspoon (5ml) Ground cinnamon

- 4 Tablespoons (60ml) Organic, natural peanut butter

- 1 Cup (250ml) Additional oat milk, for serving

Instructions:

1. Place the raw gluten-free oats, ground cinnamon and raw seeds in the dish of your slow cooker.

2. Add the sliced banana and oat milk, stir all together.

3. Stir in the peanut butter.

4. Place the lid on the slow cooker and turn to a low heat.

5. Cook overnight (approximately 8 hours)

To Serve:

1. In four separate serving bowls, place ½ cup (125ml) of the cooked oats mix into each bowl.

2. Warm the additional oat milk either in the microwave or on the stove top in a saucepan.

3. Add ¼ cup (60ml) of the warm oat milk to each bowl of oats and stir well before serving.

4. Note that heating the additional oat milk is optional.

Chocolaty Brown Rice with Hazel Nuts and Strawberries

Brown rice is naturally gluten-free and high in essential B vitamins, minerals and fiber making it another very healthy grain choice for breakfast. One wouldn't normally consider rice as a breakfast grain option, but the nutty flavor of wholegrain brown rice makes for a delicious and comforting base to a hearty breakfast. As with oat meal, brown rice is also known for its ability to lower cholesterol, and its slow releasing carbohydrate content will keep you full and satisfied all morning. Hazel nuts provide protein, healthy fats and minerals to this dish, while the strawberries and raw cocoa add essential amino acids and anti-oxidants.

Serves 4

Ingredients:

- 1 Cup (250ml) Raw Brown Rice

- 2 Cups (500ml) Oat milk

- 1 Cup (250ml) Fresh strawberries, quartered

- 4 Tablespoons (60ml) Raw Hazel nuts, finely chopped

- 1 Tablespoon (15ml) Raw cocoa powder

- 1 teaspoon (5ml) Ground cinnamon

- 1 Cup (250ml) Additional oat milk, for serving

Instructions:

1. Place the raw brown rice, ground cinnamon, raw cocoa powder and hazel nuts in the dish of your slow cooker.

2. Stir in the quartered strawberries.

3. Add the oat milk and stir well.

4. Place the lid on your slow cooker and set to a low heat.

5. Cook overnight, approximately 8 hours.

To Serve:

1. In four separate serving bowls, place ½ cup (125ml) of the brown rice mix.

2. Heat the additional oat milk in the microwave or on the stove top in a saucepan.

3. Add ¼ cup (60ml) of the warm oat milk to each bowl of brown rice mix and stir well before serving.

4. Heating of the additional oat milk is optional.

Apple Pie Gluten-Free Oatmeal with Raisins, Almonds and Coconut Cream

Apples are high in vitamin C, minerals and fiber, making them an excellent fruit choice for breakfast since they help to maintain satiety and energy levels. Raisins are a great source of iron and the cinnamon not only adds a comforting flavor, but is also known for its blood-glucose regulating properties. Waking up to the smell of this breakfast on a winter's morning will be sure to start your day with a smile.

Serves 4

Ingredients:

- 1 Cup (250ml) Raw Gluten-free Oats

- 2 Cups (500ml) Oat milk

- 1 Cup (250ml) Grated fresh apple, it is recommended that you don't peel the apple before grating it as this will add to the fiber content of the meal, as well as prevent the loss of essential nutrients that are found just underneath the skin of the fruit.

- ½ Cup (125ml) Raisins

- 1 teaspoon (5ml) Ground Cinnamon

- ½ teaspoon (2.5ml) Baking spice mix

- ¼ teaspoon (1.25ml) Ground cloves

- 1 teaspoon (5ml) Vanilla essence

- 1 Cup (250ml) Coconut Cream for serving

- 4 Tablespoons (60ml) Raw almonds, finely chopped, for serving

Instructions:

1. Place the raw gluten-free oats, baking spice mix, cinnamon, ground cloves and raisins in the dish of your slow cooker

2. Add the grated apple and stir all together

3. In a jug, mix the oat milk with the vanilla essence and add it to the oats mixture.

4. Stir well.

5. Place the lid on the slow cooker and set to a low heat

6. Cook over night, approximately 8 hours

To Serve:

1. Using four separate serving bowls, place ½ cup (125ml) of the cooked oat mixture in each bowl

2. Whip the coconut cream to a fluffy consistency

3. Add ¼ cup (60ml) coconut cream to each bowl of oats

4. Sprinkle 1 tablespoon (15ml) of the chopped almonds over each bowl and serve.

Coconuty Brown Rice Breakfast Pudding with Mango, Cashew Nuts and Dried Pineapple

The high fiber and B vitamin content of brown rice makes it a very versatile grain, so there is no reason why it can't form the basis of a wholesome and nutritious breakfast. Mangoes are high in vitamin C and are known to contain pre-biotics, so they are a great aid to the digestive system. The dried pineapple provides a zing to the overall flavor as well as some extra vitamins and minerals. The coconut and cashew nuts provide healthy fats that will round off this breakfast as a great slow-releasing, energizing meal.

Serves 4

Ingredients:

- 1 Cup (250ml) Raw brown rice

- 2 Cups (500ml) Coconut milk

- 1 Cup (250ml) Diced fresh mango

- 4 Tablespoon (60ml) Desiccated coconut

- 4 Tablespoons (60ml) Dried pineapple, finely chopped

- 1 teaspoon (5ml) Ground ginger

- 1 teaspoon (5ml) Vanilla essence

14

- 4 Tablespoons (60ml) Raw cashew nuts, roughly chopped, for serving

- 1 Cup (250mL) Coconut cream, for serving

Instructions:

1. Place the raw brown rice, ground ginger, desiccated coconut and dried pineapple into the dish of your slow cooker

2. Add the fresh mango and stir together

3. In a jug, mix the coconut milk with the vanilla essence

4. Add the coconut milk to the rice mixture and stir well

5. Place the lid on your slow cooker and cook overnight, approximately 8 hours

To Serve:

1. In four separate serving bowls, place ½ cup (250ml) of the cooked mango rice

2. Whip the coconut cream

3. Place ¼ cup (60ml) coconut cream on top of each bowl of mango rice

4. Sprinkle 1 tablespoon (15ml) of the chopped cashew nuts over each bowl and serve

Cornmeal Porridge with Dates and Seeds

Cornmeal is an excellent source of fiber and essential minerals; it also contains a small amount of healthy fats and is gluten-free. Dates are known for their high vitamin C and iron content and the raw sees add some extra heart-healthy fats to this dish. This is a great breakfast option on a day that will involve large amounts of physical activity.

Serves 4

Ingredients:

- 1 Cup (250ml) Raw cornmeal

- 2 Cups (500ml) Almond milk

- ½ Cup (125ml) Chopped dates

- ½ Cup (125ml) Raw seed mix

- 1 teaspoon (5ml) Ground cinnamon

- 1 Cup (250ml) Additional almond milk for serving

- 4 Tablespoons (60ml) Tahini, for serving

Instructions:

1. Place the raw cornmeal, chopped dates, seed mix and cinnamon into the dish of your slow cooker, stir all together

2. Add the almond milk and stir well

3. Place the lid on your slow cooker and cook on a low heat overnight, approximately 8 hours.

To Serve:

1. Using four separate serving bowls, place ½ cup (125ml) of the cooked cornmeal porridge into each bowl

2. Heat the additional almond milk in either the microwave or a saucepan on the stovetop

3. Pour 1 Tablespoon (15ml) of the Tahini over each bowl of the cornmeal porridge

4. Pour ¼ cup (60ml) of the warm almond milk over each bowl of the cornmeal porridge and stir well before serving.

5. Heating of the additional almond milk is optional

Millet with Pear and Brazil Nuts

Millet is another versatile gluten-free grain that can be enjoyed at breakfast time as well; it is known for its high magnesium content and its ability to aid in muscle tissue recovery and repair, it is also high in B vitamins. Pears are known for their high fiber content and are rich in essential vitamins and minerals. Brazil nuts not only contain heart healthy fats, but are also high in selenium and are known for their ability to help lower cholesterol.

Serves 4

Ingredients:

- 1 Cup (250ml) Raw millet

- 2 Cups (500ml) Oat milk

- 1 Cup (250ml) Diced fresh pear

- 4 Tablespoons (60ml) Raw Brazil nuts, finely chopped

- 1 Teaspoon (5ml) Ground cinnamon

- 1 Teaspoon (5ml) Vanilla essence

- 1 Cup (250ml) Additional oat milk, for serving

Instructions:

1. Place the raw millet, diced pear, brazil nuts and ground cinnamon into the dish of your slow cooker and stir together

2. In a jug, mix the oat milk with the vanilla essence

3. Add the oat milk and vanilla mixture to the millet mix and stir well

4. Place the lid on to the slow cooker

5. Cook overnight on a low heat, approximately 8 hours.

To Serve:

1. In four separate bowls, place ½ cup (125ml) of the cooked millet in each bowl

2. Heat the additional oat milk in either the microwave or a saucepan on the stove top

3. Add ¼ cup (60ml) of the warm oat milk to each bowl of millet and stir well before serving

4. Heating of the additional oat milk is optional.

"Carrot Cake" Gluten-Free Oatmeal with Pecan Nuts and Coconut Cream

Carrots are high in vitamin A and are a great source of healthy carbohydrates, anti-oxidants and essential minerals. Pecan nuts are also high in essential minerals and are known to help lower cholesterol. This is another comforting, filling breakfast option.

Serves 4

Ingredients:

- 1 Cup (250ml) Raw gluten-free Oats

- 2 Cups (500ml) Oat milk

- 1 Cup (250ml) Grated fresh carrot

- 4 Tablespoons (60ml) Raw pecan nuts, finely chopped

- ½ Cup (125ml) Golden Sultanas

- 1 teaspoon (5ml) Ground Cinnamon

- 1 teaspoon (5ml) Baking spice mix

- ½ teaspoon (2.5ml) Ground ginger

- 1 teaspoon (5ml) Vanilla essence

- 1 Cup (250ml) Coconut cream, for serving

- 4 Tablespoons (60ml) Tahini, for serving

Instructions:

1. Place the raw gluten-free oats, ground cinnamon, baking spice mix, ground ginger, pecan nuts, sultanas and grated carrot into the dish of your slow cooker, stir all together.

2. In a jug, mix the oat milk with the vanilla essence

3. Add the oat milk and vanilla mix to the oats mixture and stir well.

4. Place the lid on the slow cooker

5. Cook at a low heat overnight, approximately 8 hours

To Serve:

1. In four separate serving bowls, place ½ cup (125ml) of the carrot cake oats into each bowl

2. Whip the coconut cream

3. Top each bowl of carrot cake oats with ¼ cup (60ml) whipped coconut cream

4. Drizzle 1 tablespoon (15ml) of Tahini over each bowl and serve

PART II Lunches

In our fast-paced modern day lives we often find ourselves skipping lunch, but this is a meal that is just as important as either of the other two main meals of the day. Lunch time is when we get to take a break and re-charge our batteries in order to keep going for the rest of the day. A wholesome, nutritious and energy-sustaining meal at this time of the day is the best way to do this. The recipes in this section will give you a great midday pick-up since they all focus on providing a nutritionally balanced and filling meal that is gluten-free and that can be enjoyed hot or cold.

Quinoa with Butternut, Onion and Chickpeas

Butternut is a very versatile vegetable that is high in vitamin A and healthy carbohydrates. By cooking butternut in a slow cooker you are releasing its natural sweetness, making this dish one of those that is truly delicious either hot or cold.

Serves 4

Ingredients:

- 1 Cup (250ml) Raw Quinoa

- 4 Cups (1litre) Diced raw butternut

- 1 Can chickpeas, drained and well rinsed

- 1 teaspoon (5ml) Fresh garlic, finely chopped

- 2 medium sized onions, halved and sliced

- 1 teaspoon (5ml) Ground organic sea salt

- 1 teaspoon (5ml) Ground black pepper

- 1 teaspoon (5ml) fresh or dried rosemary

- 2 Cups (500ml) hot water

- 4 Tablespoons (60ml) Raw pumpkin seeds, for serving

Instructions:

1. Place the raw quinoa at the bottom of the dish of the slow cooker

2. In a separate bowl, mix the onions, garlic, salt, pepper, rosemary, raw butternut and chickpeas together

3. Add the butternut mix to the dish of the slow cooker

4. Add the hot water

5. Place the lid on the slow cooker

6. Cook for on a low heat for 8 hours

To serve:

1. In four separate serving bowls, place 1 cup (250ml) of the butternut quinoa dish in each bowl.

2. Sprinkle 1 tablespoon (15ml) of the raw pumpkin seeds over each bowl and serve

Egg Plant Melanzane with Black Olives and Lentils

This dish is a vegan option for the classic north Italian dish that is made up of layers of eggplant and tomatoes. By making this dish in the slow cooker you are allowing all the natural flavors, including the sweetness of the tomatoes to permeate into the eggplant and lentils. This really is a wholesome dish that can also be enjoyed hot or cold.

Serves 4

Ingredients:

- 3 large Eggplants, sliced

- 4 Cups (1litre) Fresh tomatoes, finely chopped

- 1 Can lentils, drained and well rinsed

- 1 teaspoon (5ml) Fresh garlic, finely chopped

- ½ Cup (125ml) Black olives, pitted

- 1 teaspoon (5ml) Dried Italian herb mix

- 1 teaspoon (5ml) Ground organic sea salt

- 1 teaspoon (5ml) Ground black pepper

- 1 Tablespoon (15ml) Extra virgin olive oil

- ¼ (60ml) Fresh basil leaves, finely chopped

Instructions:

1. In a bowl, mix the chopped tomatoes, garlic, dried herb mix, salt, pepper, black olives and lentils.

2. Line the base of the dish of your slow cooker with a layer of the eggplant slices

3. Cover the eggplant slices with 1 Cup (250ml) of the tomato mixture

4. Add another layer of eggplant slices

5. Add another 1cup (250ml) of the tomato mixture

6. Continue layering as such until you have used all the ingredients, but you must make sure that your top layer is one of eggplant slices

7. Drizzle the olive oil over the top and cover with the lid of the slow cooker

8. Cook on a low heat for 8 hours

To Serve:

1. Using four separate serving bowls, place a generous amount of the melanzane in each bowl

2. Sprinkle 1 tablespoon (15ml) of the fresh basil over each bowl and serve

3. It is optional to drizzle a little additional extra virgin olive oil over each bowl before serving

Mixed Vegetables with Brown Rice and Red Kidney Beans

This is a very colorful dish that is perfect for that midday pick-me-up. The variety of vegetables provides good mix of essential vitamins and minerals. Together with the brown rice and red kidney beans you have a wholesome, protein rich lunchtime meal. By cooking all these vegetables in the slow cooker you are allowing them to create their own natural stock, and flavor.

Serves 4 (but will probably have leftovers)

Ingredients:

- 1 Cup (250ml) Raw carrot, sliced

- 1 Cup (250ml) Raw cauliflower florets

- 1 Cup (250ml) Raw zucchini, sliced

- 1 Cup (250ml) Raw broccoli florets

- 1 Cup (250ml) Fresh, or frozen peas

- 1 Cup (250ml) Fresh, or frozen sweet corn kernels

- 1 Can Red kidney beans, drained and well rinsed

- 1 teaspoon (5ml) Fresh Garlic, finely chopped

- 1 teaspoon (5ml) Dried Italian herb mix

- 1 teaspoon (5ml) Ground organic sea salt

- 1 teaspoon (5ml) Ground black pepper

- 1 Cup (250ml) Raw brown rice

- 2 Cups (500ml) Hot water

- 4 Tablespoon (60ml) Raw seed mix, for serving

Instructions:

- Place the raw brown rice in the bottom of the slow cooker dish

- In a separate bowl, mix all the vegetables, red kidney beans, garlic, herbs, salt and pepper.

- Add the vegetables to the slow cooker dish

- Add the hot water

- Cover with the lid and cook on a low heat for 8 hours

To Serve:

1. Using four separate serving bowls, place 1 cup (250ml) of the cooked vegetables in each bowl.

2. Sprinkle 1 tablespoon (15ml) of the raw seed mix over each bowl and serve

Brown Rice with Tofu, Spinach, Black Olives and Red Onion

It's a well known fact that spinach is high in the essential mineral iron; it is also a very tasty and versatile leafy vegetable. Red onions are high vitamins and essential minerals, and they add a little extra color to this dish. The black olives add their unique flavor along with a dose of heart healthy fats. This dish does require a little extra pre-preparation in the form of browning the tofu and toasting the pine nuts.

Serves 4:

Ingredients:

- 4 Cups (1 liter) Fresh spinach leaves

- 4 Cups (1 liter) Firm tofu, diced

- 1 Tablespoon (15ml) Extra virgin olive oil

- ½ Cup (125ml) Black olives, pitted

- 2 Medium sized red onions, halved and sliced

- 1 teaspoon (5ml) Fresh garlic, finely chopped

- 1 teaspoon (5ml) Dried Italian herb mix

- 1 teaspoon (5ml) Ground organic sea salt

- 1 teaspoon (5ml) Ground black pepper

- 1 Cup (250ml) Raw brown rice

- 2 Cups (500ml) Hot water

- 4 Tablespoons (60ml) Raw pine nuts, for serving

Instructions:

1. First brown the tofu by heating the olive oil in a wok and frying up the tofu until it has a golden brown finish, set aside.

2. Place the raw brown rice in the bottom of the slow cooker dish

3. In a separate bowl, toss the raw spinach with the garlic, herbs, black olives, salt and pepper

4. Add tofu to the spinach mix and toss again

5. Add the tofu/spinach mix to the slow cooker dish

6. Pour over the hot water and cover with the lid

7. Cook on a low heat for 8 hours

8. While the slow cooker is going, toast the pine nuts in a dry non-stick pan until they are golden brown, set aside for garnishing the meal when serving

To Serve:

1. Using four separate serving bowls, place a desired amount of the cooked tofu, brown rice and spinach in each bowl

2. Sprinkle 1 tablespoon (15ml) of the toasted pine nuts over each bowl and serve

Cornmeal with Tomato, Butter Beans, Sweet Peppers and Black Olives

Cornmeal is a good source of essential nutrients, fiber and protein and is a very versatile gluten- free grain. The butter beans add extra protein and fiber and the combination of tomato and sweet peppers make this meal very high in vitamin C.

Serves 4

Ingredients:

- 1 Cup (250ml) Raw Cornmeal

- 4 Cups (1 liter) Raw cherry tomatoes, halved

- 4 Cups (1 liter) Mixed sweet peppers (red, yellow, orange) chopped

- 1 teaspoon (5ml) Fresh garlic, finely chopped

- ½ Cup (125ml) Black olives, pitted

- 1 teaspoon (5ml) Dried Italian herb mix

- 1 teaspoon (5ml) Ground organic sea salt

- 1 teaspoon (5ml) Ground black pepper

- 1 Tablespoon (15ml) Extra virgin olive oil

- 1 Cup (250ml) Hot water

Instructions:

1. Place the raw cornmeal on the bottom of the slow cooker dish and drizzle with the olive oil

2. In a separate bowl, mix the tomatoes, sweet peppers, butter beans, garlic, dried herbs, salt, pepper and black olives

3. Add the vegetable and butter bean mix to the slow cooker dish

4. Add the hot water

5. Cover with the lid and cook on a low heat for 8 hours

To Serve:

1. Before serving you'll need to stir the dish in order to break up the cornmeal into grains

2. In four separate serving bowls, place the desired amount of the meal and serve

3. It is optional to drizzle a little extra virgin olive oil over each bowl before serving

Ratatouille, Red Kidney Beans and Black Olives

Ratatouille is a very versatile dish that combines a variety of vegetables, making it very high in essential vitamins and minerals. This is another one of those dishes that can be enjoyed either hot or cold.

Serves 4

Ingredients:

- 1 Can Red kidney beans, drained and well rinsed

- 1 Cup (250ml) Raw egg plant, diced

- 1 Cup (250ml) Raw zucchini, sliced

- 2 Cups (500ml) Raw cherry tomatoes, halved

- 1 Cup (250ml) Mixed sweet peppers (red, yellow and orange) chopped

- ½ Cup (125ml) Black olives, pitted

- 1 Large onion, finely chopped

- 1 teaspoon (5ml) Fresh garlic, finely chopped

- 1 teaspoon (5ml) Ground organic sea salt

- 1 teaspoon (5ml) Ground black pepper

- 1 teaspoon (5ml) Dried Italian herb mix

Instructions:

1. In a separate bowl, mix the red kidney beans, eggplant, zucchini, tomatoes, sweet peppers, garlic, dried herbs, black olives, salt and pepper

2. Place the vegetables to the slow cooker dish

3. Cover with the lid and cook for 8 hours on a low heat setting

To Serve:

1. Using four separate serving bowls place the desired amount of ratatouille in each bowl and serve.

2. It is optional to drizzle a little extra virgin olive oil over each bowl before serving.

PART III Soups

Soup is one of the ultimate comfort foods and even though we tend to mainly serve them in the winter months, there is actually no reason why we can't enjoy them all year round. What makes a homemade soup such a healthy meal option is that by making it yourself you are avoiding the high sodium and preservative content of commercially made convenience soups, as well as the added gluten that is used in these products in order to thicken them and preserve their shelf life. These recipes will show how your slow cooker will turn soup making into one the most convenient and time saving ways of cooking. Soups are also easy to freeze, providing you with a healthy meal option that is quick and easy to defrost any time you need it.

Hearty Minestrone Soup

You can never go wrong with a good old minestrone soup. This recipe is packed with flavor and variety that will guarantee you a well rounded healthy, balanced meal. What makes this recipe even more appealing is that every time you heat it up, the flavor will improve.

Serves 4-8

Ingredients:

- 1 Cup (250ml) Raw carrot, diced

- 1 Cup (250ml) Raw celery, sliced

- 1 Cup (250ml) Raw turnip, diced

- 1 Cup (250ml) Raw leeks, finely chopped

- 2 Cups (500ml) Raw tomatoes, finely chopped

- 1 Cup (250ml) Raw mushrooms (these can be any variety of your choosing)

- 1 Can Red kidney beans, drained and well rinsed

- ½ Cup (125ml) Celery leaves, finely chopped

- 1 Tablespoon (15ml) Fresh coriander, finely chopped

- 1 Tablespoon (15ml) Fresh garlic, finely chopped

- 1 teaspoon (5ml) Ground organic sea salt

- 1 teaspoon (5ml) Ground black pepper

- 1 teaspoon (5ml) Dried herb mix

- 4 Cups (1itre) Hot water

Instructions:

1. Place all the vegetables and the red kidney beans in the slow cooker dish

2. Add the garlic, dried herbs, salt, pepper, celery and coriander leaves

3. Cover the vegetables with the hot water

4. Place the lid on the slow cooker and cook on a low heat setting for 8-12 hours. The longer you allow it to simmer, the better the flavor will be

To Serve:

1. Place 1 cup (250ml) of minestrone soup in each of your serving bowls

2. Serve with a whole grain, gluten-free bread of your choice

Coconuty Butternut Soup with Cashew Nuts

This is a very comforting soup to enjoy anytime on a cold winter's day. The butternut provides you with healthy carbohydrates and vitamin A, while the chick peas add the protein. The flavor of the coconut milk, combined with chilli and lime will keep you going back for more. This soup will need to be put through the blender once it is finished cooking, since it is best served with a smooth consistency.

Serves 4-8

Ingredients:

- 4 Cups (1litre) Raw butternut, diced

- 1 Can chickpeas, drained and well rinsed

- 4 Cups (1litre) Coconut milk

- 1 Tablespoon (15ml) red chilli, finely chopped

- 1 Tablespoon (15ml) Fresh garlic, finely chopped

- 1 Tablespoon (15ml) Fresh ginger, finely chopped

- 1 Tablespoon (15ml) Freshly squeezed lime juice

- 1 Tablespoon (15ml) Grated lime zest

41

- 4- 8 Tablespoons (60-120ml) Raw cashew nuts, finely chopped, for serving

- 4-8 Tablespoons (60-120ml) Coconut cream, for serving

Instructions:

1. In a bowl, mix the butternut, chickpeas, garlic, chilli, lime zest and ginger together

2. Place the butternut mixture in the slow cooker dish

3. Add the coconut milk and lime juice, stir well

4. Place the lid on the slow cooker

5. Cook at a low heat setting for at least 10 hours, until the butternut is so soft that it is falling apart

6. Once the soup has cooled enough, place it in a blender or food processor and blend until smooth

7. Return the soup to the slow cooker dish and turn it onto a high heat until the soup comes back to a simmer and is hot enough to serve

To Serve;

1. Place 1 cup (125ml) of the butternut soup into each serving bowl

2. Swirl 1 tablespoon (15ml) of coconut cream over the center of each bowl

3. Sprinkle 1 tablespoon (15ml) of the chopped cashew nuts over the coconut cream swirl of each bowl

4. Serve with a whole grain gluten-free bread of your choice

Roasted Sweet Pepper and Tomato Soup with Lentils

With the main ingredients of this soup being the sweet peppers and tomatoes, it is very high in vitamin C, making it an excellent choice for winter. This soup does require a little pre-preparation in the form of roasting the peppers, but it really is so worth it as it brings out the sweetness of the peppers. This is also another soup that will be best served with a smooth consistency and so will require blending once it is cooked.

Serves 4-8

Ingredients:

- 4 Cups (1 liter) Mixed sweet peppers, chopped

- 4 Cups (1 liter) Cherry tomatoes, halved

- 1 Can lentils, drained and well rinsed

- 1 Tablespoon (15ml) Extra virgin olive oil

- 1 Tablespoon (15ml) Fresh garlic, finely chopped

- 1 Tablespoon (15ml) Fresh basil leaves, finely chopped

- 1 Teaspoon (5ml) Fresh, or dried rosemary

- 1 Teaspoon (5ml) Ground organic sea salt

- 1 Teaspoon (5ml) Ground black pepper

- 4 Cups (1litre) Hot water

- 4-8 Tablespoons (60-120ml) Black olives, pitted, for serving

Instructions:

1. Preheat the oven to 350 degrees (200 degrees Celsius)

2. Place the chopped peppers, tomatoes, garlic, basil, rosemary, salt and pepper into a roasting dish and drizzle over the olive oil

3. Roast the vegetables in the oven for 1 hour

4. When the hour is done, turn the oven off and allow the vegetables to cool in the oven

5. Once all has cooled, place the vegetables into the slow cooker dish

6. Add the lentils

7. Add the hot water

8. Cover with the lid and cook for 8-10 hours

9. Once the soup has cooled, place it into a blender or food processor and blend until smooth

10. Return the soup to the slow cooker dish and set on a high heat until the soup returns to a simmer and is hot enough to serve

To Serve:

1. Pour 1 cup (250ml) of the soup into each serving bowl

2. Top each bowl of soup with 1 tablespoon (15ml) of the black olives

3. This soup is best served with olive gluten-free ciabatta bread, but can be served with any whole grain gluten-free bread of your choice.

PART IV Dinners

Dinner time is a special time of the day because it generally is the only meal time that the whole family can share. The recipes in this section will give you inspiration to use your slow cooker for one of its most convenient uses; having dinner ready when you walk in the door at the end of the day. The wholesome, well balanced meal options that follow will ensure your family is well fed and sustained for long fast of sleeping. All these recipes are gluten-free so you can rest assured that they won't be causing any night time tummy trouble.

Tofu Curry with Pineapple and Cashew Nuts

Coming home to the smell of this coconuty curry at the end of the day will be sure to have your stomach growling before you even open the front door. This recipe does require some pre-preparation in the form of browning the tofu. In this instance it's best to cook the rice separately, but if that's all you have to do when you get home, then this is still an easy and convenient dinner option.

Serves 4

Ingredients:

- 4 Cups (1litre) Firm tofu

- 1 Tablespoon (15ml) Organic coconut oil

- 1 Cup (250ml) Raw carrot, sliced

- 1 Cup (250ml) Raw green beans, julienned

- 1 Cup (250ml) Raw cauliflower florets, finely sliced

- 1 Cup (250ml) Fresh pineapple, diced

- ½ Cup (125ml) Spring onion, finely chopped

- 1 Teaspoon (5ml) Fresh garlic, finely chopped

- 1 Teaspoon (5ml) Fresh ginger, finely chopped

- 1 Teaspoon (5ml) Fresh red chilli, finely chopped

- 1 Teaspoon (5ml) Fresh green chilli, finely chopped

- ½ Cup (125ml) Whole raw cashew nuts

- 4 Cups (1 litre) Coconut Milk

- 4 Tablespoons (60ml) Freshly squeezed lime juice

- 1 Tablespoon (15ml) Grated lime zest

- 1 Cup (250ml) Brown Rice

- 2 Cups (500ml) Boiling water

- 1 Teaspoon (5ml) Salt

- 4 Tablespoons (60ml) Desiccated coconut, for serving

Instructions:

1. First brown the tofu by heating the coconut oil in a wok or frying pan, once the oil is hot add the tofu and fry until golden brown and slightly crispy.

2. Place the vegetables, chillies, cashew nuts, pineapple, lime zest, ginger and garlic the dish of your slow cooker

3. Add the browned tofu and stir all together

4. Add the coconut milk and lime juice, stir all together

5. Place the lid on the slow cooker and set to a low heat

6. Cook for 6-8 hours

To cook the brown rice:

1. Boil the kettle

2. Place the brown rice in a saucepan and add the salt

3. Pour the 2 cups (500ml) of boiling water over the rice, cover the saucepan with the lid and bring it to the boil

4. Once the rice is boiling, turn the heat down and let it simmer at a low heat until the rice has absorbed all the water and is light and fluffy, this will take about 45-50 minutes.

To Serve:

1. In four separate serving bowls, place ½ cup (125ml) of the cooked brown rice in each bowl

2. Add 1 Cup (250ml) of the curry to each bowl

3. Sprinkle 1 tablespoon (15ml) of the desiccated coconut over each bowl and serve

Vegetable Curry with Dried Apricots and Red Kidney Beans

This curry is inspired by the traditional cooking of the Cape Malay culture of South Africa. The unique blend of spicy and sweet creates a hearty and comforting dinner. The combination of ingredients makes this a very nutritious and well balanced meal that will be a great dinner option at any time of the year. This dish can be served with either brown rice or quinoa, and it is best to cook the grain of your choice separately.

Serves 4

Ingredients:

- 1 Cup (250ml) Raw sweet potato, diced

- 1 Cup (250ml) Raw butternut, diced

- 1 Cup (250ml) Raw cauliflower florets, sliced

- 1 Can Red kidney beans, drained and well rinsed

- 1 Cup (250ml) Dried apricot halves

- 1 Tablespoon (15ml) Apricot jam or preserve

- 1 large onion, finely chopped

- 1 Tablespoon (15ml) Coconut oil

- 1 Teaspoon (5ml) Fresh garlic, finely chopped

- 1 Teaspoon (5ml) Fresh ginger, finely chopped

- 1 Teaspoon (5ml) Ground cinnamon

- 1 Teaspoon (5ml) Gluten-free Masala curry spice mix

- ½ Teaspoon (2.5ml) Cumin Seeds

- ½ Teaspoon (2.5ml) Ground coriander

- 1 Cup (250ml) Brown rice or quinoa

- 2 Cups (500ml) Boiling water

- 1 Teaspoon (5ml) Salt

- 4 Tablespoons (60ml) Desiccated coconut, for serving

Instructions:

1. Heat the coconut oil in a frying pan and add the onion, garlic, ginger, cinnamon, gluten-free Masala mix, cumin seeds and ground coriander. Fry all together until the onion turns transparent

2. Turn the heat of the pan down to medium and add the apricot jam, stirring constantly until the jam has become slightly runny in consistency and has coated the onion mixture. Remove from the heat and set aside

3. Place the vegetables, red kidney beans and dried apricots into the dish of the slow cooker

4. Add the onion mixture and stir well

5. Place the lid on the slow cooker and set to a low heat

6. Cook for at least 8 hours

To cook the brown basmati rice or quinoa:

1. Boil the kettle

2. Place the brown rice or quinoa in a saucepan and add the salt

3. Add 2 Cups (500ml) of boiling water to the saucepan and bring to the boil

4. Turn the heat down to low and allow the grain of choice to simmer until all the water has been absorbed and it is light and fluffy.

To Serve:

1. Using four separate serving bowls, place ½ cup (125ml) of the cooked rice or quinoa in each bowl

2. Add 1 Cup (250ml) of the curry to each bowl

3. Sprinkle 1 tablespoon (15ml) of desiccated coconut over each bowl and serve

Vegetable Pot Pie

This meal has it all, the variety of vegetables, healthy slow-releasing carbohydrates, protein and fats, which makes it the perfect dinner option the night before a very active day, or sporting event. This vegetable pie is also very delicious served cold as a left-over for lunch.

Serves 4-8

Ingredients:

- 1 Cup (250ml) Raw brown rice

- 1 Can Red kidney beans, drained and well rinsed

- 1 Large sweet potato, sliced (it is not necessary to peel the potatoes, as this adds to the rustic feel of the dish)

- 1 Cup (250ml) Raw butternut, diced

- 2 Cups (500ml) Raw button mushrooms, sliced

- 1 Cup (250ml) Raw cherry tomatoes, halved

- 1 Cup (250ml) Fresh or frozen peas

- 1 Cup (250ml) Fresh or frozen sweet corn kernels

- 1 medium onion, finely chopped

- 1 Cup (125ml) Black olives, pitted and halved

- 1 Teaspoon (5ml) Fresh garlic, finely chopped

- 1 Teaspoon (5ml) Dried Italian herb mix

- 1 Teaspoon (5ml) Ground organic sea salt

- 1 Teaspoon (5ml) Ground black pepper

Instructions:

1. Place the raw brown rice in the base of the slow cooker dish

2. Cover the rice with the mushrooms

3. Cover the mushrooms with the tomatoes and red kidney beans

4. In a separate bowl, mix the onion, garlic, dried herb mix, salt and pepper, and spread it over the tomato layer

5. Cover the tomato layer with the peas and sweet corn kernels

6. Cover the pea and sweet corn layer with the black olives

7. Lastly layer the sliced sweet potato over the top of the dish

8. Place the lid on the slow cooker and turn on to a low heat

9. Cook for at least 10 hours

To Serve:

1. Place 1 Cup (250ml) of the vegetable pot pie in each serving bowl, making sure that each serving consists of all the layers of the pie.

2. It is optional to drizzle a little extra virgin olive oil over the top of each serving

Pumpkin Pie with Chickpeas and Buckwheat

Buckwheat is gluten-free grain that is high in fibre and is a great source of magnesium, it is also well known for its blood sugar regulating properties, making it a great dinner time choice in order to avoid the midnight hunger pangs. This makes for a very comforting meal. Pumpkin is high in essential minerals and healthy carbohydrates, the pumpkin seeds provide a concentrated source of protein, vitamins and minerals as well. This is another of those dishes that can be enjoyed hot or cold, so any leftovers make a great lunch box meal.

Serves 4-8

Ingredients:

- 4 Cups (1litre) Raw pumpkin, finely diced

- 1 Can chickpeas, drained and well rinsed

- 1 Cup (250ml) Raw buckwheat

- 1 Tablespoon (15ml) Ground cinnamon

- 4 Tablespoons (40ml) Tahini, for serving

- 4 Tablespoons (40ml) Raw pumpkin seeds, for serving

- 4 Tablespoons (40ml) Raw sunflower seeds, for serving

Instructions:

1. Place the raw buckwheat in the base of the slow cooker dish

2. In a separate bowl, mix the pumpkin with the chickpeas and ground cinnamon

3. Add the pumpkin and chickpea mix to the slow cooker dish, making sure that all the couscous is covered with the pumpkin mix

4. Place the lid on the slow cooker and set to a low heat

5. Cook for 10 hours

To Serve

1. Using separate serving bowls, place approximately 1 cup (250ml) of the pumpkin pie in each bowl, making sure that each serving includes the buckwheat from the bottom of the pie.

2. Drizzle 1 tablespoon (15ml) of Tahini over each bowl

3. Sprinkle 1 tablespoon (15ml) of the raw pumpkin seeds over each bowl

4. Sprinkle 1 tablespoon (15ml) of the raw sunflower seeds over each bowl

5. Serve

Black Mushroom, Lentil and Potato Bake

Black mushrooms have a distinct flavor that makes them a delicious addition to any recipe, the black fungus is known to improve circulation and lower cholesterol. Potatoes are a great source of healthy carbohydrate, and are incredibly versatile since they take on and enhance the other flavors of this dish.

Serves 4-8

Ingredients:

- 4 large potatoes, sliced (it is not necessary to peel the potatoes, as this gives the dish a rustic feel)

- 4 Cups (1 liter) Black mushrooms, sliced

- 1 Can lentils, drained and well rinsed

- 1 Teaspoon (5ml) Fresh garlic, finely chopped

- 1 Teaspoon (5ml) Dried Italian herb mix

- 1 Teaspoon (5ml) Dried or fresh rosemary

- 1 Teaspoon (5ml) Ground Organic sea salt

- 1 Teaspoon (5ml) Ground black pepper

- 1 large onion, finely chopped

- 1 Tablespoon (15ml) Extra virgin olive oil

Instructions:

1. In a bowl, mix the sliced mushrooms, lentils, chopped onion, garlic, herbs, salt and pepper

2. Line the dish of the slow cooker with a layer of sliced potato

3. Cover the first layer of potato with 1 cup (250ml) of the mushroom mix

4. Cover the layer of mushroom mix with another layer of sliced potato

5. Cover the sliced potato with another cup (250ml) of the mushroom mix

6. Continue to layer as such until you have used all your ingredients, making sure that your top layer is one of potato.

7. Drizzle the olive oil over the top layer

8. Place the lid on the slow cooker and set to a low heat

9. Cook for 8 to 10 hours

To Serve:

1. Place 1 cup (250ml) of the mushroom potato bake into each serving bowl

2. It is optional to drizzle a little extra virgin olive oil over each bowl before serving.

Teff Bake with Mushrooms, Zucchini and Black Olives

Teff is another gluten-free grain that is very high in calcium and is also an excellent source of vitamin C, which is not usually a vitamin found in grains. The slow releasing carbohydrate content of this dish will keep your whole family satisfied throughout the night. This is another versatile meal that can be enjoyed hot or cold and so any leftovers will make a great lunch box meal.

Serves 4-8

Ingredients:

- 1 Cup (250ml) Raw teff

- 1 Cup (250ml) Black mushrooms, sliced

- 1 Cup (250ml) White button mushrooms, sliced

- 1 Cup (250ml) Zucchini, sliced

- 1 Cup (250ml) Fresh cherry tomatoes, halved

- 1 Can Butter beans, drained and well rinsed

- 1 Cup (250ml) Fresh or frozen peas

- 1 Cup (250ml) Fresh or frozen sweet corn kernels

- 1 Cup (250ml) Black olives, pitted and sliced

- 1 Teaspoon (5ml) Fresh garlic, finely chopped

- 1 Large onion, finely chopped

- 1 Teaspoon (5ml) Dried Italian herb mix

- 1 Teaspoon (5ml) Fresh or dried rosemary

- 1 Teaspoon (5ml) Ground organic sea salt

- 1 Teaspoon (5ml) Ground black pepper

- 4 Tablespoons (60ml) Raw pine nuts

Instructions:

1. Place the raw teff in the base of the slow cooker dish, you might have to break it up a little to make it fit

2. In a bowl mix the mushrooms, zucchini, tomatoes, butter beans, peas, corn, black olives, onion, garlic, herbs, salt and pepper.

3. Place the vegetable mix on top of the spaghetti in the slow cooker dish

4. Cover the dish with its lid and set to a low heat

5. Cook for 8-10 hours

6. Toast the raw pine nuts in a dry non-stick pan until they have darkened in color

To Serve:

1. Place 1 cup (250ml) of the mushroom teff into each serving bowl

2. Sprinkle 1 tablespoon (15ml) of the toasted pine nuts over each bowl and serve

Curried Rice and Lentil Bake

This dish is inspired by the traditional Hindi dish of biryani. It is a warm and comforting meal that is high in slow releasing carbohydrates, healthy fats and protein. This recipe provides another meal option that can be enjoyed hot or cold, making the leftovers a great option for a lunchbox. This is a rather spicy dish, so if you're not too keen on the heat then you can leave out the chillies and only use the gluten-free Masala mix

Serves 4-8

Ingredients:

- 2 Cups (500ml) Raw Brown rice

- 1 Cup (250ml) Raw potato, diced

- 1 Can lentils, drained and well rinsed

- 1 Cup (250ml) Fresh or frozen sweet corn kernels

- 1 Cup (250ml) Raw Carrot, diced

- 1 Cup (250ml) Fresh or frozen peas

- 1 Cup (250ml) Button mushrooms, sliced

- 4 Cups (1litre) Hot water

- 1 Tablespoon (15ml) Fresh garlic, finely chopped

- 1 Tablespoon (15ml) Fresh ginger, finely chopped

- 1 Teaspoon (5ml) Fresh red chilli, finely chopped

- 1 Teaspoon (5ml) Fresh green chilli, finely chopped

- 1 Teaspoon (5ml) Gluten-free Mild Masala mix

- ½ Teaspoon (2.5ml) Cumin seeds

- 1 Teaspoon (5ml) Ground coriander

- 4 Tablespoons (60ml) Extra Virgin Coconut oil

- 4 Tablespoons (60ml) Raw Seed mix, for serving

- 4 Tablespoons (60ml) Fresh coriander, finely chopped, for serving

- 4 Tablespoons (60ml) Gluten-free Fruit chutney, or organic apricot jam for serving

Instructions:

1. In a bowl, mix the raw basmati rice, potato, lentils, carrots, peas, corn, mushrooms, ginger, garlic, chillies, Masala mix, cumin seeds and coriander

2. Toss in the coconut oil

3. Place all the mixed ingredients into the dish of the slow cooker

4. Add the hot water and stir all together

5. Place the lid on the slow cooker and set to a low heat

6. Cook for 10 to 12 hours, ideally the rice will have absorbed all the water and will be light and fluffy

To Serve:

1. Place 1 cup (250ml) of the rice and lentil bake into each serving bowl

2. Pour 1 tablespoon (15ml) of the gluten-free fruit chutney or organic apricot jam over each serving

3. Sprinkle 1 tablespoon (25ml) of the raw seed mix over each bowl

4. Sprinkle 1 Tablespoon (15ml) of the fresh chopped coriander over each bowl and serve.

Bonus Recipe: Gluten-Free Slow Cooker Bread

Given the fact that this recipe book has an entire section dedicated to gluten-free soup recipes for your slow cooker, it seems that the book just wouldn't be complete without including a recipe for gluten-free bread that can be enjoyed with any one of those soup recipes. This bread recipe is easy to make and can be done so by using any one of the gluten-free flours that are available in most health food stores. These gluten-free flours are:

- Almond Flour

- Buckwheat Flour

- Corn Flour

- Garbanzo Bean Flour

- Millet Flour

- Oat Flour

- Potato Flour

- Soy Flour

- Quinoa Flour

- Rice Flour

- Sorghum Flour

- Teff Flour

In this instance of the recipe, we will be using corn flour.

Serves 8-10

Ingredients:

- 4 Cups (1kg) Corn Flour

- 3 Cups (750ml) Lukewarm Water

- 1 Tablespoon (15ml) Organic sea salt

- 1 Tablespoon (15ml) Instant dry yeast

- 2 Tablespoons (30ml) Raw organic brown sugar

- 3 Tablespoons (45ml) Extra Virgin Olive oil

Instructions:

1. In a glass measuring jug or bowl, dissolve the raw organic brown sugar into the lukewarm water

2. Sprinkle the instant dry yeast over the top of the sugar and water mixture, cover with cling film and set aside for approximately 30 minutes until the yeast has begun to bubble and is well activated.

3. Weigh out the flour and sift it into a large mixing bowl

4. Add the salt to the flour

5. Once the yeast mixture has begun to bubble, add it to the flour

6. Using your hands mix the flour and water/yeast mixture together until it begins to form a dough

7. Turn the dough out onto a lightly floured surface and knead for approximately ten minutes until the dough is smooth and elastic and is no longer sticking to your fingers.

8. Place the dough back into the mixing bowl, cover with cling film and a warm, damp dish cloth. Set aside in a warm place for approximately one hour or until the dough has doubled in size

9. Using the three tablespoons (45ml) of extra virgin olive oil, grease the dish of your slow cooker

10. Once the dough has risen and doubled in size, turn it out onto a lightly floured surface and knead it for another five minutes.

11. Place the dough into the dish of your slow cooker, making sure you press it out to fill all the corners and completely cover the base of the dish

12. Place the lid on your slow cooker and turn the heat up to high

13. Bake the bread for approximately six to eight hours or until it sounds hollow when tapped with the knuckles on the top of the loaf

14. Once the bread is baked, turn off the slow cooker and allow it to cool

15. Once the bread is cool, turn it out onto a wire cooling rack until completely cold before slicing as desired.

BONUS RECIPES: Green Smoothies: Green Smoothies for Weight Loss and Health

Watermelon Smoothie
Serves 1-2

Ingredients

- 1 cup of water melon
- ¾ cup of blue berries
- 1 banana
- ½ cup of kale
- 1 teaspoon barley grass
- ½ broccoli

Directions

1. Peel the banana the night before you want to make the smoothie.
2. Put the cut banana in the freezer overnight.
3. Cut the rind off the watermelon and make sure you take the seeds out as well.
4. Cut the water melon into cubes.
5. Put the watermelon in the blender.
6. Add the blueberries and barley grass to the blender.

7. Pull the leaves off the stems of the kale.

8. Add the banana and the kale to the mixture.

9. The broccoli can be put into the blender raw, but it sometimes tastes better if you cook the broccoli first.

10. You can try the smoothies both ways and decide which one you like.

11. Cut the broccoli away from any big stems.

12. But up the broccoli and throw it into boiling water.

13. Let it simmer for no more than five minutes.

14. Cook the broccoli just until it is soft.

15. This allows for the most amount of nutrients to stay in the broccoli.

16. Put the broccoli raw or cooked in the blender with the rest of the ingredients and blend together on low to medium.

17. When the mixture is blended well, serve in a glass with a straw.

Honeydew Chia Berry Smoothie
Serves 1-2

Ingredients

- 1 cup honeydew melon
- 1 date
- ½ cup of apple juice
- ½ fresh then frozen raspberries
- ½ cup of spinach
- ½ chia seed powder
- 1 teaspoon lemon

Directions

1. Put the fresh raspberries in a freezer appropriate container and place the container in the freezer the night before.
2. When you are ready to make the smoothie take the raspberries out of the freezer.
3. Cut up the honeydew melon and make sure to cut the hard skin from the honeydew melon.
4. Spoon out the seeds before measuring the melon into a cup.
5. Cut the pit out of the date.
6. Pour the ½ cup of apple juice into the blender.
7. Put the date and the honeydew melon into the blender.
8. Then put the frozen raspberries and lemon juice into the blender.

9. Make the chia seed powder in a coffee grinder by grinding the chia seeds.

10. Measure out the spinach leaves and put the spinach and the chia seed powder into the blender.

11. Blend all the ingredients on low to medium.

12. Make sure everything is blended well.

13. Taste to make sure you like.

14. Gradually add more of one or more ingredients if you need to.

15. Pour smoothie in a glass with a straw.

Very Berry Smoothie

Serves 1-2

<u>Ingredients</u>

- 1 cup of fresh then frozen raspberries
- ½ cup of fresh then frozen strawberries
- 2 teaspoons chlorophyll
- 1 cup of cold coconut milk
- ½ cup of kale
- ½ cup of blueberries

<u>Directions</u>

1. Wash the strawberries and raspberries and place them into the freezer overnight.
2. In the morning pour the cold coconut milk into the blender.
3. Take the kale leaves off of the stems.
4. Add the chlorophyll, kale, and blueberries to the blender.
5. Blend all the ingredients together on low to medium speed.
6. Make sure that all ingredients are well blended.
7. Taste and make sure you like the smoothie.
8. If you need to gradually add one or more of the ingredients to the taste.
9. When you are ready pour the smoothie into a glass and serve with a straw.

Pear Smoothie

Server 1-2

Ingredients

- 2 pears
- 1 teaspoon cinnamon
- ½ cup of cashew milk
- ½ cup of apple juice
- ½ cup of melon

Directions

1. Take the two pears wash them and cut the skins off of the outside of the pears.
2. Cut the pears in half and cut the pear meat away from the core of the pear.
3. Put the pear meat into the blender.
4. Measure the ½ teaspoon of cinnamon and put into the blender.
5. Add the cashew milk, apple juice, and melon.
6. Mix all the ingredients together on a low to medium speed.
7. Mix until the ingredients are well blended.
8. Taste your smoothie and gradually add a small amount of ingredients if need.
9. When you like the taste of the smoothie pour the smoothie into a glass with a straw and serve.

Ginger Smoothie

Serves 1-2

Ingredients

- 2 teaspoons ginger
- 2 dates
- ½ cup of kale
- ½ cup of apple juice
- Juice of half of a lemon

Directions

1. Take the ginger and cut the skin from the outside.
2. Take the dates and cut the pit from the center of the dates.
3. Put the ginger and dates into the blender.
4. Pull the kale leaves away from the core.
5. Put the kale in the blender and pour in the apple juice as well.
6. Squeeze the juice of the lemon into a glass and make sure to take out all of the seeds. Then pour the lemon into the blender.
7. Mix all the ingredients in the blender on a low to medium speed.
8. Make sure everything is blended well and copped up as much as possible.
9. Taste and adjust for desired taste if you need to.
10. Pour the smoothie into a glass and serve with a straw.

Cocoa Mint Smoothie

Serves 1-2

Ingredients

- ¼ cup of fresh mint
- ½ cup of cold almond milk
- 1 tablespoon of cocoa powder
- 1 banana

Directions

1. Peel the banana and cut it in half.
2. Put the banana in the freezer in a freezer appropriate container the night before making the smoothie.
3. Wash the mint and cut the mint as small as you can.
4. Pour the almond milk in the blender.
5. Put the mint, the tablespoon of cocoa powder, and the frozen banana in the blender. Blend on low to medium until all the ingredients are as small as they can be and everything is blended well.
6. Taste and adjust if you need to.
7. Pour the smoothie into a glass and drink with a straw.

Chamomile Kale Smoothie

Serves 1-2

Ingredients

- 1 cup of chamomile tea
- ½ cup of almond milk
- ½ banana
- ½ cup of kale
- 2 date
- 2 tablespoons nutritional yeast

Directions

1. Buy a strong healthy good quality chamomile tea.

2. Make a cup and put two tea bags in so that the chamomile gets a nice and strong flavor. Put the chamomile tea in the refrigerator so it cools before you make the smoothie.

3. You can make the tea the night before.

4. When it is time to make the smoothie pour the almond milk in the blender.

5. Peel the banana and add it to the blend.

6. Pull the kale leaves away from the stems and add ½ cup of kale to the mix.

7. Cut the dates in half and remove the pits.

8. Put the nutritional yeast and dates into the blender.

9. Mix all the ingredients in the blender until they are all well mixed.

10. All the ingredients should be in the smallest form possible.

11. Taste and adjust smoothie by gradually adding one or more ingredients if you need to.

12. When the smoothie is ready pour it into a glass and serve smoothie with a straw.

Olive Oil Green Smoothie
Serves 1-2

Ingredients

- 1 tablespoon olive oil
- ½ cup of apple juice
- ½ cup of broccoli
- ½ cup of artichokes
- ½ cup of kale
- ½ cup of arugula
- 1 pear
- Dash of salt

Directions

1. Cook the broccoli so it is soft.
2. Buy artichokes in a glass container.
3. Add olive oil, apple juice, broccoli, and artichokes to the blender and mix on low to medium.
4. Then pull the kale leaves from the kale stems.
5. Cut the pear in half and peel away the skin.
6. Then cut away the core and stem.
7. Put pear meat and the kale into the blender and mix on low to medium.
8. Put the dash of salt in with the ingredients.
9. Mix all the ingredients until they are all in small pieces and the liquid is smooth to drink. Taste and adjust if you need

to. When the smoothie is ready pour the smoothie into a glass with a straw.

Lavender Strawberry Smoothie
Serves 1-2

Ingredients

- 1 teaspoon of culinary lavender
- 2 cups of water
- 2 sprigs of mint
- ½ cucumber
- ½ cup of Strawberries
- 1 teaspoon Spirulina

Directions

1. In a large glass jug add the teaspoon of culinary lavender and the 2 cups of water.
2. Put the two sprigs of mint into the jug.
3. Put in the refrigerator for two hours and take out the sprig of mint.
4. Then keep the lavender mixture in the refrigerator for three more hours.
5. Then strain the lavender from the water.
6. Add lavender water to the blender.
7. Peel the cucumber and measure out ½ cup of cucumber meat and put it in the blender. Cut the green leaves off of the strawberries.
8. Also add the strawberries and Spirulina to the blender.

9. Mix all the ingredients together until smooth and well blended.

10. Taste and adjust if you need to.

11. Serve the smoothie in a glass cold with a straw to drink.

Vanilla Smoothie

Serves 1-2

Ingredients

- 1 natural vanilla bean
- ½ cup of cashew milk
- ½ banana
- 2 tablespoons nutritional yeast
- ½ cup of kale

Directions

1. Take the vanilla bean and press it flat with your fingers.
2. Then take a knife and gently split the vanilla bean open and scoop out the fresh vanilla specs with a spoon.
3. Pour the cashew milk into the blender.
4. Peel the banana and put the banana into the blender.
5. Then put the vanilla and the nutritional yeast in the mix.
6. Also separate the kale leaves from the stems and add the kale to the blender as well. Turn the speed on low and gradually use medium in order to blend all the ingredients together.
7. Blend the mix well so everything is pureed. When smoothie is at desired flavor, pour the smoothie into a glass and serve with a straw.

Cinnamon Smoothie

Serves 1-2

Ingredients

- 2 teaspoons of cinnamon
- ½ cup of almond milk
- 1 apple
- ½ cup of broccoli
- 1 teaspoon barley grass

Directions

1. Cook the broccoli just until it is soft.
2. Pour the almond milk in the blender.
3. Add the ingredients of cinnamon and broccoli along with the barley grass.
4. You can buy fresh cinnamon sticks and grate the cinnamon sticks with a grater until you have enough to fill two teaspoons.
5. Take the peel off of the apple and remove the seed, stem, if it has one, and the core.
6. Put the apple meat into the blender.
7. Turn the blender speed to low and gradually raise to medium.
8. Mix all of the ingredients together until well blended.
9. Taste your smoothie and adjust if you need to by adding a small amount of one or more of the ingredients.

10. When you have your desired flavor, pour the smoothie into a glass and serve with a straw.

Ashwagandha Coconut Smoothie
Serves 1-2

<u>Ingredients</u>

- 1 teaspoon of Ashwagandha powder
- ½ coconut milk
- 1 frozen banana
- 1 apple
- 3 dates
- ½ cup of blue berries
- ½ teaspoon of lime juice

Directions

1. Warm up the coconut milk in a stainless steel pan on a medium heat.
2. Add the Ashwagandha powder to the warm milk and stir while it is on a low heat.
3. Put the mixture in the refrigerator to cool.
4. You can make the Ashwagandha and coconut mix the night before.
5. Peel the apple and remove the stem and core.
6. Remove the pits from the dates and put the dates in the blender.
7. Add also the lime and apple meat.
8. Mix all the ingredients on a low to medium speed.
9. Mix them well so that all the flavors mix together.
10. Try the smoothie and add a little of one or more ingredients if it needs it.
11. When the smoothie is ready pour the smoothie into a glass with a straw.

Don't forget to download...

Your Free Gift

You will find more amazing smoothie recipes in "Vegan Superfood Smoothie Recipes" eBook. Yes, it's free! Grab your copy now:

www.bitly.com/karenfreegift

If you have any problems with your download, email me at:
karenveganbooks@gmail.com

Conclusion

Thank you for reading!

I hope that with so many vegan recipes you will be motivated and inspired to start and/or continue your journey towards vibrant health and total wellbeing.

Remember, the beauty of incorporating nutritious vegan foods into your daily diet is that you are making simple, yet sustainable changes that will work for your health long-term. These solutions are eco-friendly and cruelty-free.

If you enjoyed my book, it would be greatly appreciated if you left a review so others can receive the same benefits you have. Your review can help other people take this important step to take care of their health and inspire them to start a new chapter in their lives.

At the same time, <u>you can help me serve you and all my other readers</u> even more through my next vegan-friendly recipe books that I am committed to publishing on a regular basis.

I'd be thrilled to hear from you. I would love to know your favorite recipe(s).

Don't be shy, post a comment on Amazon! Your comments are really important to me.

→ Questions about this book? Email me at: karenveganbooks@gmail.com

Thank You for your time,

Love & Light,

Until next time-

Karen Vegan Greenvang

www.amazon.com/author/karengreenvang

More Vegan Books by Karen

Available in kindle and paperback in all Amazon stores.

Made in the USA
San Bernardino, CA
22 September 2016